DINO

Bites

priddy books

D1501812

DINOSAURS RULE!

Long, long ago, there were **no people**, no horses or rabbits, and no cats, rats, or bats. But there were **DINOSAURS!** They were the **biggest** and most **fierce** animals that ever lived on land.

Tail

Scaly skin

Ears to hear

Nose for smelling

Good eyesight

Strong muscles

Tongue for tasting

Teeth

Bendable neck

Carnivore: Carnotaurus

The first known bird, Archaeopteryx, lived 150 million years ago. It was very similar to small meat-eating dinosaurs.

Foot claws

What is a dinosaur?

Dinosaurs were close cousins of crocodiles and alligators. They were also related to lizards and snakes, turtles and tortoises. They had a skeleton of bones, a tail, scaly skin, and lots of teeth!

Archaeopteryx

Omnivore: Gallimimus

Some dinosaurs were herbivores and ate plants. Others, the carnivores, ate meat—especially other dinosaurs! Some dinosaurs ate almost anything, and they were called omnivores.

The Age of Dinosaurs
(Dates correct at time of publication)

252 million years ago

66 million years ago

Triassic Period
Dinosaurs first existed during a time called the Triassic Period, which lasted from 252 to 201 million years ago.

Jurassic Period
They grew bigger and spread around the world during the Jurassic Period, 201 to 145 million years ago.

Cretaceous Period
The greatest of all dinosaurs lived during the Cretaceous Period, from 145 to 66 million years ago.

Troodon

Guess what? In one way, it's STILL the Age of Dinosaurs. Some small meat-eating dinosaurs similar to Troodon changed and became the first birds. So experts say dinosaurs are still alive—as birds.

I found this in my dress-up box!

Grrrr!

3

Use your glow-in-the-dark pieces to make an awesome dinosaur skeleton! Use this template as a guide.

Use multipurpose tack to stick this onto your wall!

4

TYRANNOSAURUS REX

Tyrannosaurus rex, or T. rex, is one of the best known and most **popular** dinosaurs. It was a **fierce** carnivore, with **powerful** running legs, **huge** teeth, and **strong jaws.**

1

Find the dino sticker on every fact page!

Not all experts agree, but it is possible T. rex could run as fast as 25 mph. That's about the same as a world-class human sprinter—so YOU would have NO chance!

WOW! He's tall!

T. rex had very tiny arms. No one knows what it used them for.

Arm wrestle, anyone?

A museum paid almost $8 million for the fossil skeleton of a T. rex named Sue.

If you think a T. rex made a mighty roar, think again. It is more likely to have grumbled like a crocodile, or shrieked like an eagle!

Grumble, grumble!

A T. rex tooth could be almost 12 inches long. That's one BIG tooth to brush!

T. rex was a fearsome predator. It could eat up to 500 lbs of meat in one bite. That's the same size as a small zebra!

What?!?!

FACT FILE

How to say it:
Ty-RAN-oh-sor-russ Rex

What the name means:
Tyrant lizard king

Throughout, we compare the dinosaurs to an adult!

How big?
40 ft long, 20 ft tall

Meat-eater or vegetarian?
Meat-eater

Triassic, Jurassic, Cretaceous?
Cretaceous, 68–66 million years ago

Where in the world?
North America

STEGOSAURUS

"**Steggy**" was a strange creature known as a "plated" dinosaur. It had tall **slabs** of lightweight, triangular-shaped bone **sticking up** from its back. There were two rows, one slightly **behind** the other. You wouldn't want to mess with those!

Not as comfy as a pillow!

Its biggest back plates were almost as big as your pillowcase!

The teeth of Stegosaurus were small and quite weak. It could only eat soft plants, and probably had to chew all day to get enough food.

What were the back plates for?

Showing off
Maybe they were bright and colorful, to say, "Look at me, I'm the boss!"

Keeping cool or staying warm
If Stegosaurus got too hot, it could give off heat, like a radiator, or if it got too cold, soak up the sun's heat, like a solar panel.

Protection
The plates protected the main body from predator bites.

But there are problems with all these ideas. The short answer is: No one truly knows.

How to say it:
Steg-oh-sor-russ

What the name means:
Roof or covered-over lizard

How big?
30 ft long, 3 ft tall

Meat-eater or vegetarian?
Vegetarian

Triassic, Jurassic, Cretaceous?
Jurassic, 155–150 million years ago

Where in the world?
North America, Europe

For its big, bulky body, Stegosaurus had a tiny head containing an even tinier brain—probably smaller than your fist!

2

The long, sharp tail spikes were a fearsome defense weapon called a thagomizer. Just right for swinging at big meat-eating dinosaurs to break their legs!

BIG TEETH vs BIG HORNS

SPECIAL SKILLS

T. rex had a great sense of smell, which may have helped it to hunt at night.

T. rex

SIZE: 40 ft long

WEIGHT: 7 tons

ATTACK WEAPONS: More than 50 strong teeth in crunching jaws, big foot claws

DEFENSE WEAPONS: Powerful swishy tail

Think I could do with a pedicure!

Triceratops could lower its head and charge like a dino-rhino!

Triceratops

SIZE: 28 ft long

WEIGHT: Up to 10 tons

ATTACK WEAPONS:
Sharp beaklike mouth, long head horns

DEFENSE WEAPONS:
Protective neck frill

Do you like my frill?

WHO'S THE WINNER IN THIS BATTLE OF THE DINO MEGA-BEASTS? FLIP OVER TO PAGE 54 TO FIND OUT!

11

MIX AND MATCH

Can you find the stickers and match the pairs of dinosaurs?

3

Hadrosaurus

Zephyrosaurus

Ouranosaurus

4

Lesothosaurus was the smallest of these dinosaurs.

5

Lesothosaurus

Brachiosaurus was the **biggest** of these dinosaurs.

Brachiosaurus

6

7

9

8

Coelophysis

And I'm the coolest.

Tuojiangosaurus

Lesothosaurus is looking for his friends. Help him find a way through the maze!

Start

Finish

DEINONYCHUS

About as tall as a person, **Deinonychus** was swift and **sneaky**—a high-speed **hunter** of smaller creatures. It was in the dinosaur group called **raptors**, which means "**thief**" or "grabber."

10

Its long jaws had 60 sharp curved teeth, and it could bite faster than you blink.

Its hands were big and strong, with three fingers tipped with sharp claws to grab prey.

It had a big, sharp, curved claw on its second toe that easily sliced through flesh.

Some Deinonychus fossils show several of them together. They may have gathered around a big, dead dinosaur to have a shared feast.

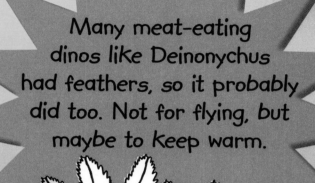

Many meat-eating dinos like Deinonychus had feathers, so it probably did too. Not for flying, but maybe to keep warm.

FACT FILE

How to say it:
Day-non-ee-kuss

What the name means:
Terrible claw

How big?
10 ft long, 5 ft high

Meat-eater or vegetarian?
Meat-eater

Triassic, Jurassic, Cretaceous?
Cretaceous, 115–110 million years ago

Where in the world?
North America

Brr, it's cold!

TRICERATOPS

Biggest of the horned dinosaur group, **Triceratops** was also one of the **last** of all the big dinosaurs. It **lived** and **died** right at the **end** of the Cretaceous Period.

The neck frill or shoulder shield was solid bone, so it probably weighed almost one ton—nearly as much as a family mini car.

The two big eyebrow horns were 3 feet long and used to stab enemies or poke rivals in the herd at breeding time.

There were no teeth at the front of the mouth. Instead, Triceratops had a sharp curved beak like a parrot's, which it used to easily snip through twigs and branches.

11

Triceratops had one of the biggest skulls of any land animal, measuring 8 feet long—bigger than your bed!

When fossil hunters first found the horns of Triceratops, in 1887, they thought they were from a giant bison!

Say what?!?

A fossil of a baby Triceratops skull has also been found. It's just 3 feet long, with big eyes and short horns. What a cutie!

FACT FILE

How to say it:
Try-serra-tops

What the name means:
Three-horned face

How big?
28 ft long, 10 ft tall

Meat-eater or vegetarian?
Vegetarian

Triassic, Jurassic, Cretaceous?
Cretaceous, 68–66 million years ago

Where in the world?
North America

SPEEDY VS SLOWCOACH

SPECIAL SKILLS
Deinonychus was fast, agile, and good at leaping.

Deinonychus

SIZE: 10 ft long

WEIGHT: 150 lb

ATTACK WEAPONS:
Sharp teeth, hand claws, big toe claw

DEFENSE WEAPONS:
Swiping tail

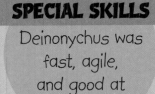

Ankylosaurus

SPECIAL SKILLS
Ankylosaurus squatted down to protect its underside.

SIZE: 30 ft long

WEIGHT: 7 tons

ATTACK WEAPONS: Heavy, lumpy tail club

DEFENSE WEAPONS: Hard, bony armor almost all over

I'm not moving!

WHICH DINOSAUR WON THIS EPIC CONTEST?
TURN TO PAGE 54 TO FIND OUT!

COLORING: ALLOSAURUS

COLORING: TROODONS

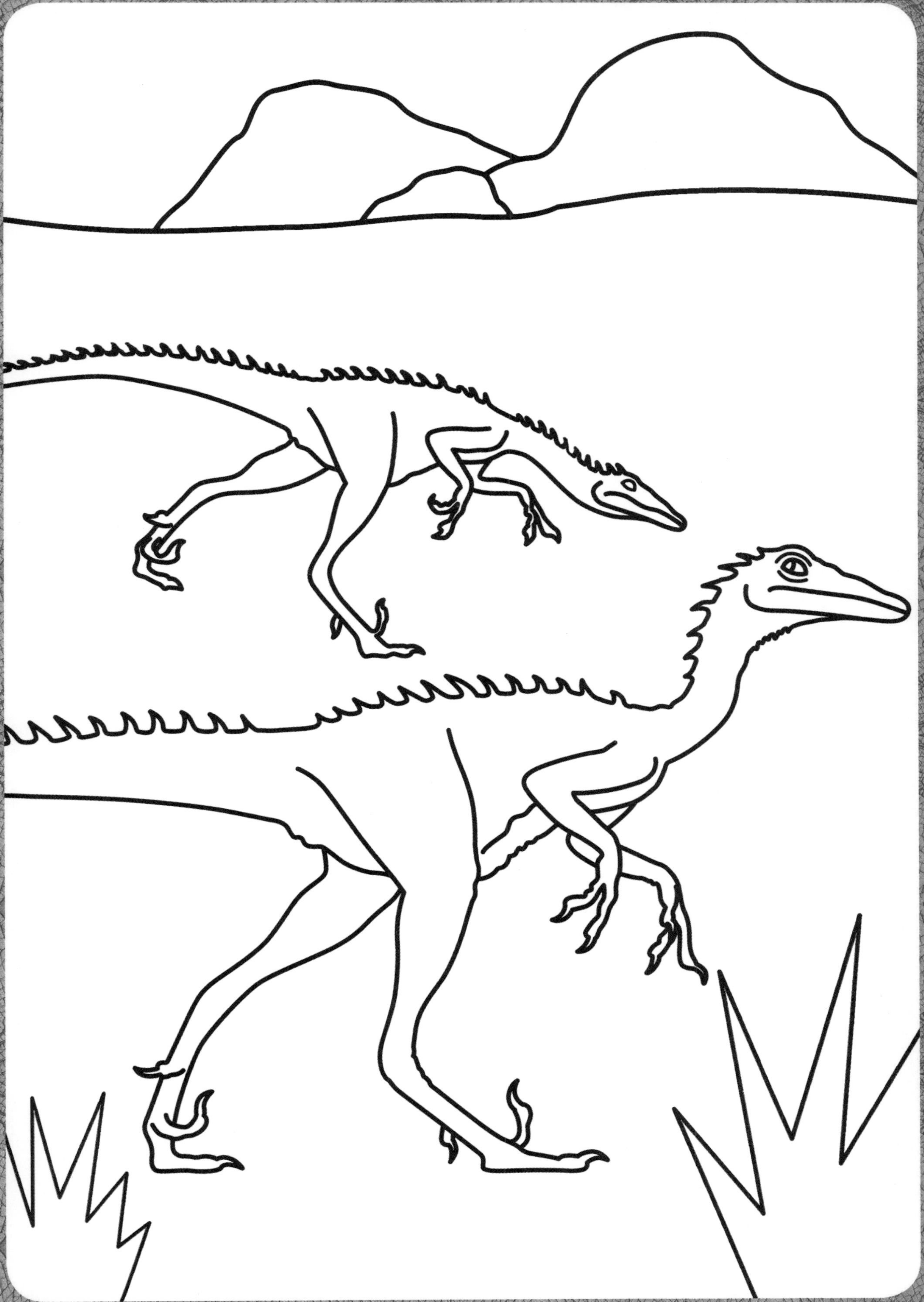

DIPLODOCUS

"Dippy" is one of the most **famous** dinosaurs, and also one of the **longest**. But most of it was a thin neck and an even **thinner** tail. It weighed only 15 tons—but that's still the same as two **elephants**!

The tail was almost half of Diplodocus's total length. The end could be cracked like a dino-whip to make a loud noise, or flicked at enemies to hurt them.

The name "double beam" comes from two ski-like parts, chevrons, on the base of each tail bone.

12

A really good fossil skeleton of Diplodocus was found in about 1900. Many copies in plaster were made and sent to museums around the world. No wonder "Dippy" is so famous!

ROAR NEWS

MOST FAMOUS DINOSAURS

With its quite long legs and slim body, Diplodocus was probably quite speedy and galloped as fast as you run!

Now look here! If Diplodocus could crane its neck up, it would have been perhaps 35 feet tall—around twice the height of a giraffe.

Who are you calling shorty?

The head of Diplodocus was so small, it had to eat all day and most of the night to take in enough nourishment. Its peglike teeth simply pulled leaves off trees to swallow—no chewing.

Diplodocus didn't just swallow food. It also gulped down stones, called gastroliths. Because it could not chew, the stones helped to mush up and mash down the plants in its stomach.

FACT FILE

How to say it:
Dip-lod-eee-kuss
(OR Dip-low-doe-kuss!)

What the name means:
Double beam

How big?
100 ft long, 25 ft tall

Meat-eater or vegetarian?
Vegetarian

Triassic, Jurassic, Cretaceous?
Jurassic, 155–150 million years ago

Where in the world?
North America

I rock!

PARASAUROLOPHUS

With one of the longest dinosaur names, **Parasaurolophus** also had the longest **crest**—the length of bone sticking up from its head. This was up to **6 feet** long—taller than you!

13

Large backward-curving head crest

Pebbly textured skin

Parasaurolophus had a wide, flat, toothless front to its mouth, like a duck's beak. That's why it belonged to the dinosaur group called hadrosaurs or "duckbills."

Quack! Quack!

FACT FILE

How to say it:
Parra-sor-oh-loaf-uss

What the name means:
Near crested lizard

How big?
30 ft long, 14 ft tall

Meat-eater or vegetarian?
Vegetarian

Triassic, Jurassic, Cretaceous?
Cretaceous, 75–73 million years ago

Where in the world?
North America

Its beak was okay to gather plant food, but it could not chew. So Parasaurolophus had hundreds of big, sharp-edged teeth in its cheeks, for super-strong chewing. Check-ups at the dentist would take a very long time!

What about a game of hoops?!

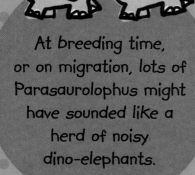

At breeding time, or on migration, lots of Parasaurolophus might have sounded like a herd of noisy dino-elephants.

What was the head crest for?

Snorkel to breathe underwater
An old idea, but not true—there was no hole at the top!

Showing off
Possible—the bigger and older Parasaurolophus grew longer crests, which impressed herd rivals.

Making noise
Also possible—air passing up and down inside could make it vibrate like a trombone.

Parp!

Can you find all the dinosaur words in the word search? There are eight to find!

t	r	i	c	e	r	a	t	o	p	s
m	a	c	r	o	p	l	a	t	a	o
t	e	s	n	e	i	l	w	n	r	e
r	b	t	t	a	o	o	a	c	w	o
o	m	e	e	s	i	s	s	c	i	s
o	p	e	e	r	o	a	r	l	u	m
d	y	t	s	r	e	u	t	a	f	e
o	a	h	l	e	a	r	o	w	l	p
n	q	e	t	h	u	u	n	t	e	t
r	u	n	s	l	i	s	a	m	h	b
s	p	i	n	o	s	a	u	r	u	s

Triceratops   Roar   Troodon   Claw

Spinosaurus   Allosaurus   Macroplata   Teeth

28

EUOPLOCEPHALUS

Few dinosaurs were as protected as **Euoplocephalus**. It had **bony** plates, cones, spikes, and **shields** on almost every body part. Between them were hard lumps, as **small** as peas. **Bite** through that!

14

Euoplocephalus did not like hard foods. Its teeth were tiny— smaller than your little fingerprint!

Euoplocephalus was in the ankylosaur or armored dinosaur group. Its big, heavy, lumpy, swinging tail club could give a hammer blow to any enemy.

Take off Euoplocephalus's outer armor and it would lose one-fifth of its whole weight. That's like you taking off five jackets!

In 1897, the first fossils of Euoplocephalus were called Stereocephalus. Then someone noticed a little beetle already had that name, so in 1910 it was changed.

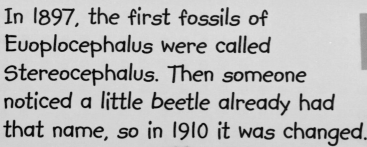

I didn't like that name anyway!

Ha!

Euoplocephalus was so heavy, it probably moved slowly. But not as slow as today's tortoise.

FACT FILE

How to say it:
You-oh-ploe-keff-ah-luss

What the name means:
Well-armed head

How big?
20 ft long, 8 ft tall

Meat-eater or vegetarian?
Vegetarian

Triassic, Jurassic, Cretaceous?
Cretaceous, 77–75 million years ago

Where in the world?
North America

Lots of small bony plates covered the front of the nose, with one large plate in the upper middle of the nose. Even the eyelids were hard and tough!

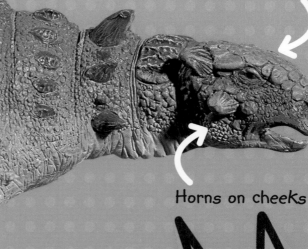

Horns on cheeks

Can you draw lines to match each creature to its special skin marking?

Macroplata

Coelophysis

Hadrosaurus

Troodon

Lesothosaurus

1. What is your favorite food?
   a) hamburger and fries
   b) spaghetti and meatballs
   c) a healthy salad
   d) nachos

Check your answers in the circles!

2. What is the hobby you enjoy the most?
   a) skateboarding
   b) chess
   c) reading
   d) watching movies with friends

3. What pet would you pick?
   a) dog
   b) gecko
   c) fish
   d) cat

4. In your group of friends, you are. . . .
   a) the center of attention
   b) the joker
   c) the shy one
   d) the talkative one

Mostly As
Spinosaurus was a huge predator. It may have even been the largest meat-eating dinosaur ever to have lived!

You're like Spinosaurus because. . . .
You are brave, independent, and never give up.

Mostly Bs
Troodon was an intelligent hunter. Its brain was so big, it would have been top of the class if dinosaurs went to school!

You're like Troodon because. . . .
You are quick, clever, and like to be challenged.

5. What is your favorite sport?
  a) swimming
  b) track
  c) tennis
  d) soccer

6. What do you like to do in your spare time?
  a) anything sporty
  b) extra studying
  c) chill out by yourself
  d) hang out with friends

7. What job would you like to do?
  a) firefighter
  b) doctor
  c) teacher
  d) TV host

8. Which type of movie do you prefer to watch?
  a) an action movie
  b) sci-fi
  c) something animated
  d) a comedy

Mostly Cs
Apatosaurus was a giant herbivore. These dinosaurs grew up to 90 feet—that's longer than two school buses!

You're like
Apatosaurus because. . . .
You're thoughtful, trustworthy, and calm in a crisis.

Mostly Ds
Parasaurolophus probably lived in herds. Scientists believe that they used their crests to make trumpeting noises to talk to each other.

You're like
Parasaurolophus because. . . .
You are funny, friendly, and a bit of a chatterbox!

TROODON

A small speedy hunter, **Troodon** was in the raptor or "**thief**" dinosaur group. For its size, it had very **big** eyes and a big **brain**, too. It was probably a **clever** little dinosaur.

15

With its slim body, grabbing hands, strong legs, and long tail, Troodon could race around. It twisted and darted after small food such as mammals, lizards, small birds, and bugs.

Like other raptors, Troodon's main weapon was the big, curved claw on each second toe. Usually this was held up while walking, so it stayed sharp.

1. Troodon was named in 1856 from just one fossil—its tooth!

2. In 1932, fossils similar to Troodon were called Stenonychosaurus, "narrow claw lizard."

3. In 1987, experts decided they were so similar, they WERE Troodon, so all Stenonychosaurus fossils were renamed.

4. But, with other fossils added in too, now there may be too many different ones named Troodon. Start again!

Troodon's watching you! Its big eyes could see well, probably even in twilight. They faced forward, which also allowed them to judge distances. So beware, prey!

Compared to other dinosaurs, Troodon's brain was unusually large, which was much bigger in proportion to the rest of its body. Scientists believe this made it a bit of a smartypants!

Troodon females laid around two eggs per day for over a week, meaning each had around 16–24 in the cluster, or clutch, of eggs. Eggcellent!

FACT FILE

How to say it:
True-oh-don

What the name means:
Wounding tooth

How big?
8 ft long, 4 ft tall

Meat-eater or vegetarian?
Meat-eater

Triassic, Jurassic, Cretaceous?
Cretaceous, 75–70 million years ago

Where in the world?
North America

BEIPIAOSAURUS

Never "**high-five**" a therizinosaur, or scythe-dinosaur, like **Beipiaosaurus**. It had **massive**, long, sharp finger **claws** that could easily stab and slice **flesh** to ribbons!

16

Short hairy or fiberlike feathers over most of the body, about 1 to 2 in long

What do you think?

Bigger, long strands, more like ribbons, about 1/8 in wide and up to 6 in long

Beipiaosaurus's feathers are a mystery. They were not suited for flight. Did they keep this strange dinosaur warm in cold weather? Or have bright colors to attract a mate? Or do you have an idea?

Beipiaosaurus was named after the Chinese city of Beipiao, near where its fossils were found in 1996. The person who discovered them was a farmer, Li Yinxian, who then became quite famous.

Beipiaosaurus or "Bippy" had no teeth at the front of its mouth, and small, peg-shaped teeth at the back. It probably ate soft plants.

The hand claws were sharp and curved, each one longer than your fingers.

"Bippy" lived around 125 million years ago. Its closest cousins were not plant-eating dinosaurs, but small meat-eaters like Troodon.

FACT FILE

How to say it:
Bay-p-yah-oh-sor-uss

What the name means:
Lizard from Beipiao

How big?
7 ft long, 3 ft tall

Meat-eater or vegetarian?
Probably vegetarian

Triassic, Jurassic, Cretaceous?
Cretaceous, 125 million years ago

Where in the world?
East Asia

SPECIAL SKILLS

Allosaurus could open its mouth super-wide to slash and stab victims. Yikes!

Allosaurus

SIZE: 33 ft long

WEIGHT: 3 tons

ATTACK WEAPONS:
Over 70 sharp, back-curved teeth

DEFENSE WEAPONS:
Strong, hard-kicking feet with blunt claws

Apatosaurus

SPECIAL SKILLS

A young Apatosaurus could rear up to run on its back legs. Clever!

SIZE: Up to 100 ft long

WEIGHT: 25 tons

ATTACK WEAPONS: Long, whippy tail

DEFENSE WEAPONS: Massive feet to kick and trample

Whee!

WHICH OF THESE JURASSIC MONSTERS CAME OUT ON TOP? RACE ON TO PAGE 55 TO FIND OUT!

MATCHING HEADS

Find the stickers, then draw a line between each dino and its matching head.

17

18

Baryonyx

Allosaurus

Coelophysis

19

20

21

Velociraptor

22

Tyrannosaurus rex

Carnotaurus

23

Euoplocephalus

Troodon

24

25

Tuojiangosaurus

Nodosaurus

26

27

Triceratops

IN THE SKIES AND SEAS

During the Age of Dinosaurs, no big dinosaurs **soared** in the sky or **lived** in the sea. But many great **reptiles** did. They were all **predators**, searching for prey to **grab** and swallow. **Delicious!**

In the sky were reptiles called pterosaurs, which means "winged lizard." Their front legs had become wings of thin skin, held out mainly by the long, slim bones of just one finger—the fourth one.

Pterosaurs started out small with long tails. Dimorphodon lived about 190 million years ago in Europe. Its tiny teeth were probably for snapping at little creatures, such as dragonflies and bugs.

DID YOU KNOW?

Pterosaurs liked the beach! Many lived along coasts, perched on cliffs, and swooped to snatch fish from the ocean surface.

Pteranodon

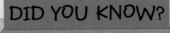

Wingspan: **20 ft**

As time went by, pterosaurs lost their long tails and got bigger . . . and bigger . . . Pteranodon swooped over North America 85 million years ago. It had a tall, pointed head crest like a witch's hat.

Dimorphodon

Wingspan: **4 ft**

In the sea swam many kinds of fierce reptiles. Some were really huge hunters, bigger even than dinosaur meat-eaters like T. rex. They feasted on fish, squid, and the coil-shelled, ammonites which died out long ago.

DID YOU KNOW?

Mosasaurs have close living relatives. These are the monitor lizards, like the Nile monitor and the fearsome Komodo dragon.

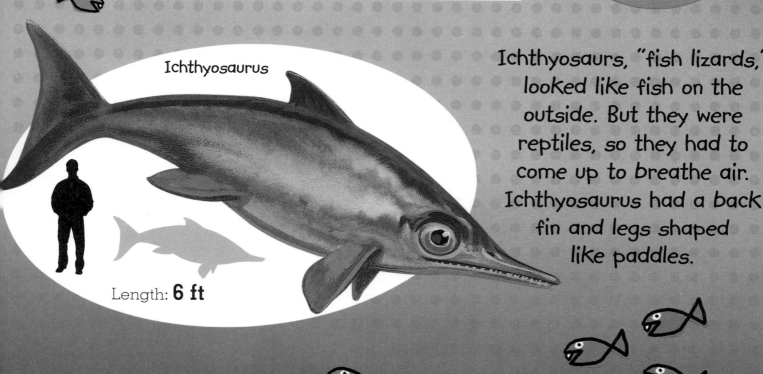

Ichthyosaurus

Length: **6 ft**

Ichthyosaurs, "fish lizards," looked like fish on the outside. But they were reptiles, so they had to come up to breathe air. Ichthyosaurus had a back fin and legs shaped like paddles.

Mosasaurs, "Meuse lizards," lived toward the end of the Age of Dinosaurs. Mosasaurus's massive head had wide jaws lined with dozens of ultra-sharp teeth to grab slippery, wriggling food.

Mosasaurus

Length: **60 ft**

QUETZALCOATLUS

One of the biggest-ever **flying** animals, the pterosaur **Quetzalcoatlus** was the size of a **four-seater** plane. It would darken the **skies** as it flew past with slow, **whooshing** wing-flaps.

28

How did Quetzalcoatlus feed?

• It soared down to peck at dead dinosaur bodies, like vultures do today. Perhaps.

• It could have swooped down to skim the water's surface and grab fish. Probably not.

• It walked along, pecking up small animals, like a giant version of the stork bird. Probable.

The bones were hollow to save weight so that this monster could fly. It probably weighed ten times more than the heaviest flying birds today.

WHOA!

What big wings you have!

The beak of Quetzalcoatlus was much bigger than you. So was the head, and the neck, and each wing bone, and almost every other body part.

A "hand" with claws along the front of the wing was Quetzalcoatlus's front foot when walking.

How to say it:
Ket-zal-koe-at-luss

What the name means:
After a mythical Aztec bird-snake god

How big?
35 ft wingspan

Meat-eater or vegetarian?
Meat-eater, scavenger

Triassic, Jurassic, Cretaceous?
Cretaceous, 68–66 million years ago

Where in the world?
North America

The first remains of Quetzacoatlus were found in Texas.

The vast wings were a sandwich of skin on the outside with thin muscle and stretchy fibers between. Like elastic, they shrank smaller when Quetzalcoatlus folded its wing bones.

Computer versions of Quetzalcoatlus show it could fly as fast as 80 mph and soar at height for perhaps 5,000 miles.

PLESIOSAURUS

Plesiosaurs were sea **reptiles** that lived during the **Age of Dinosaurs**. Some were **smaller** than you; others reached 50 feet long. They flapped their **flippers** fast to chase other sea creatures.

Like some dinosaurs described earlier, Plesiosaurus swallowed seabed pebbles (gastroliths) into its stomach. This helped it to dive more easily. If it got too heavy, it coughed them up again.

COUGH MIXTURE

29

FASTEST

Their swimming speed was thought to be 5 mph—this is about as fast as a human champion swimmer!

Plesiosaurus's four legs became paddles. But they probably did not move to and fro, like oars. They flapped up and down and tilted, like bird wings, to "fly" through the water.

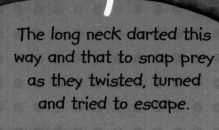

The long neck darted this way and that to snap prey as they twisted, turned and tried to escape.

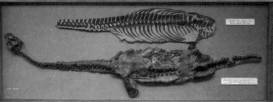

Lots of sharp teeth allowed Plesiosaurus to grab and hold scaly fish and slithery squid.

WHAT?!

Plesiosaurus fossils were among the first of long-dead reptiles to be pictured in scientific books, in the early 1700s—long before dinosaurs were named in 1842.

FACT FILE

How to say it:
Please-ee-oh-sor-russ

What the name means:
Near lizard

How big?
12 ft long

Meat-eater or vegetarian?
Meat-eater

Triassic, Jurassic, Cretaceous?
Cretaceous, 195–175 million years ago

Where in the world?
Europe

Did Plesiosaurus have babies at sea, like Ichthyosaurus and modern dolphins? Or did it crawl onto the beach to lay eggs, like a sea turtle? Sadly, no one knows.

We don't know either!

SAIL-BACKED COMBAT

Spinosaurus

SPECIAL SKILLS

Spinosaurus used its sail to warm up rapidly in the morning—for fast attack!

SIZE: 15 ft long

WEIGHT: 12 tons

ATTACK WEAPONS:
Long, low jaws with cone-shaped teeth

DEFENSE WEAPONS:
Strong, muscular tail

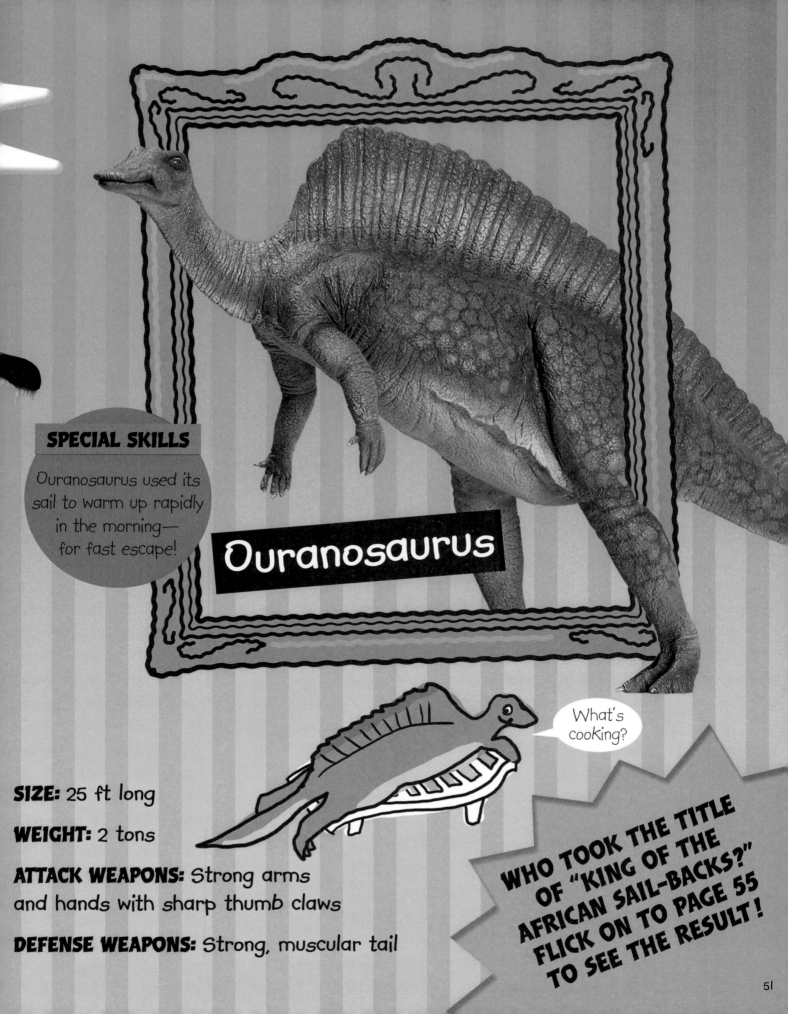

SPECIAL SKILLS

Ouranosaurus used its sail to warm up rapidly in the morning— for fast escape!

Ouranosaurus

What's cooking?

SIZE: 25 ft long

WEIGHT: 2 tons

ATTACK WEAPONS: Strong arms and hands with sharp thumb claws

DEFENSE WEAPONS: Strong, muscular tail

WHO TOOK THE TITLE OF "KING OF THE AFRICAN SAIL-BACKS?" FLICK ON TO PAGE 55 TO SEE THE RESULT!

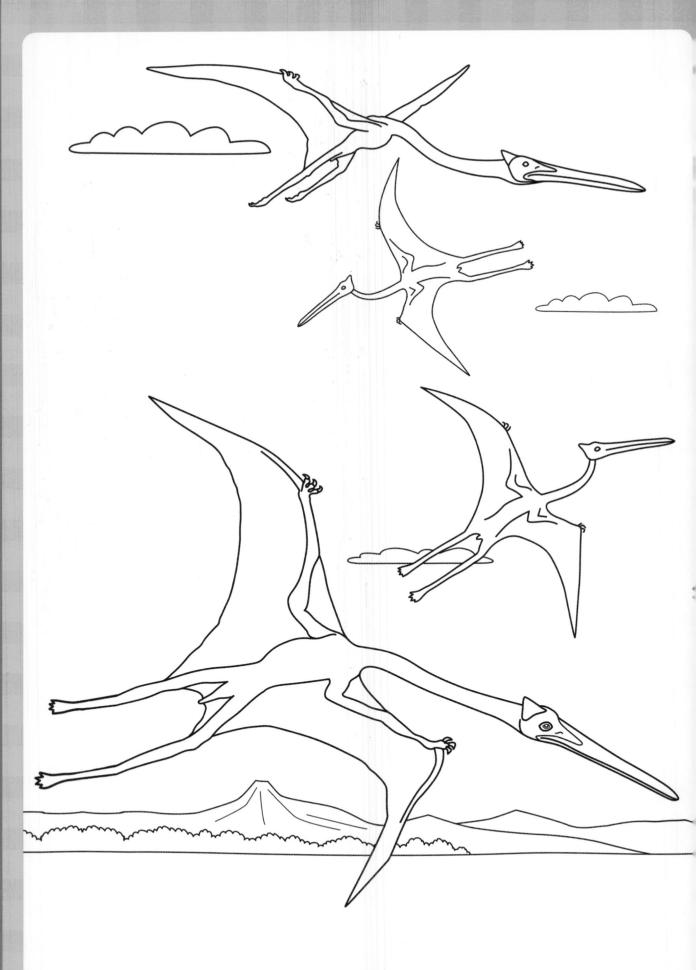

First, make sure you read all the previous pages in this book—but not the quiz below. Then come back and take the test to see if you are a dinosaur expert.

1. Dinosaurs lived through three time periods. Which was the middle one?
   - a Cretaceous
   - b Triassic
   - c Jurassic

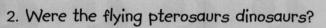

2. Were the flying pterosaurs dinosaurs?
   - a yes
   - b some of them were
   - c no

3. Which dinosaur was slowest?
   - a Diplodocus
   - b Troodon
   - c Euoplocephalus

4. How long was Deinonychus?
   - a 30 ft
   - b 20 ft
   - c 10 ft

5. Which bone held out most of the pterosaur's wing?
   - a finger bone
   - b arm bone
   - c hand bone

6. Could T. rex run faster than you?
   - a yes
   - b no
   - c about the same

7. Parasaurolophus was in which dinosaur group?
   - a duck-bills
   - b bone-heads
   - c raptors

8. Plaster copies of which dinosaur were sent to many museums around the world?
   - a Troodon
   - b Triceratops
   - c Diplodocus

9. What does the name Stegosaurus mean?
   - a door lizard
   - b roof lizard
   - c wall lizard

10. Which these ate squid and fish?
   - a Beipiaosaurus
   - b Dimorphodon
   - c Mosasaurus

THE ANSWERS ARE NOT FAR AWAY. IN FACT, THEY ARE JUST THREE PAGES AWAY!

DINO BATTLE WINNERS

T.REX VS TRICERATOPS

It was a close call. We know they actually fought, because fossils of Triceratops's neck frill have bite marks that exactly fit Tyrannosaurus's teeth. Triceratops managed to stab Tyrannosaurus with its sharp head horn. Wounded and bleeding, the meat-eater had to retreat. But on another day, who knows?

It's the TRICERATOPS!

DEINONYCHUS VS ANKYLOSAURUS

Ankylosaurus was so slow, it could not run away from speedy Deinonychus. But it was also much bigger and heavier, and threatened to crush Deinonychus. The meat-eater tried biting but the plant-eater's all-over armor was too hard. And today, no others from its hunting pack turned up to help. So Deinonychus went hungry. . . .

It's the ANKYLOSAURUS!

ALLOSAURUS VS APATOSAURUS

Allosaurus tried opening its mouth wide to jab Apatosaurus on its legs and belly, ripping open big wounds. The enormous long-neck kicked out and whipped its tail. But the predator had wisely chosen a victim who was slow and sick with old age. Before long, Apatosaurus weakened from blood loss, and Allosaurus began its huge feast.

GOLD

It's the ALLOSAURUS!

SPINOSAURUS VS OURANOSAURUS

Spinosaurus set an ambush. It waited among trees and rushed out as Ouranosaurus wandered past. The surprised plant-eater turned to face the greatest land killer the world has known. Ouranosaurus pretended to jump left, then suddenly went right. But Spinosaurus was cunning. Its huge, long jaws closed with a crunch on the sail-back's neck, whose struggles soon ended.

It's the SPINOSAURUS!

GOLD

ANSWERS TO QUIZ

Page 14

Page 28

Page 32
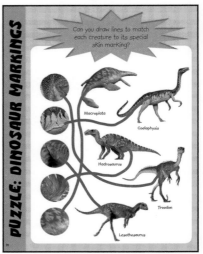

Page 53: How well do you know your dinosaurs:
1c 2c 3c 4c 5a 6a 7a 8c 9b 10c.

CREDITS

Insides: p. 6-7, 28-29: Tyrannosaurus rex © leonello calvetti / Alamy; p. 7: Burchell's zebra © ChrisKrugerSA / iStock / Thinkstock, Male runner © PCN Photography / Alamy; p. 9: Two pillows © karam miri / iStock / Thinkstock; p. 19: Wild buffalo © hinzundkunz / iStock / Thinkstock; p. 21: Ankylosaurus © Naz-3D / iStock / Thinkstock; p. 27: Dental jaw model © luchschen / iStock / Thinkstock, Diving mask © nito100 / iStock / Thinkstock, Brass trombone © Nerthuz / iStock / Thinkstock; p. 34: Dinosaur © Levent Konuk / iStock / Thinkstock, Apatosaurus © XiaImages / iStock / Thinkstock; p. 37: Troodon tooth © The Natural History Museum / Alamy; p. 38-39: Dinosaurier beipiaosaurus © Friedrich Saurer / Alamy; p. 40: Dinosaurs illustration © English School / The Bridgeman Art Library / Getty Images; p.44: Pterosaur dimorphodon / MR1805 / iStock / Thinkstock; p. 45: Mosasaurus swimming © DEA PICTURE LIBRARY / De Agostini Picture Library / Getty Images; p. 47: Speedometer © allanswart / iStock / Thinkstock; p. 48-49: Plesiosaurus © edit: Corey Ford / Stocktrek Images / Getty Images, Boat oar © Mega__Pixel / iStock / Thinkstock, Plesiosaurus conybeari © The Natural History Museum / Alamy; p. 50: Dinosaur spinosaurus © Ralf Kraft / Hemera / Thinkstock.

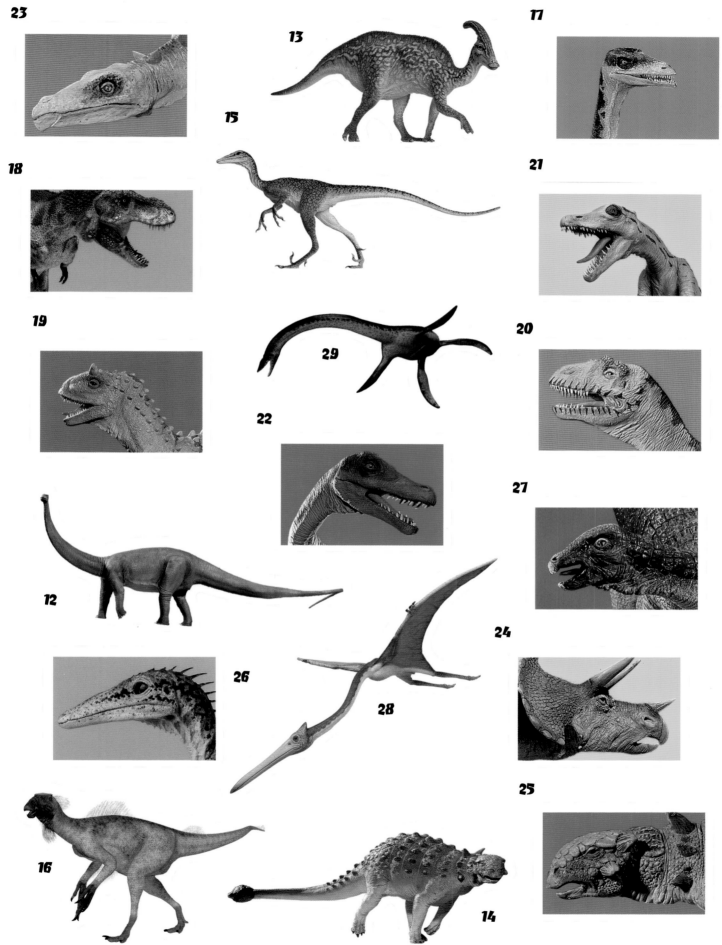

23

13

17

18

15

21

19

29

20

22

27

12

26

28

24

16

14

25

Add these fun stickers inside the book, or wherever you want!